LIFE
OBSERVATIONS

A Small Book of Verse

BARBARA WEBB

PAGE PUBLISHING
Conneaut Lake, PA

First originally published by Page Publishing 2022

ISBN 979-8-88654-348-3 (pbk)
ISBN 979-8-88654-353-7 (hc)
ISBN 979-8-88654-350-6 (digital)

Printed in the United States of America

In honor of my parents, Lydia and Erik Larson,
Who taught me the values that guide my life.

And in honor of my "Second Parents,"
Evelyn and Howard Webb,
I miss you.

To my husband, John Robert Webb,
My best friend who always encourages and supports me.

To my brother, John Larson,
The best brother ever.

To my former Juneau-Douglas high school classmates,
Who said "Publish your writing,"
and this book is the result.

And in memory of Joseph Timothy "Tim" Whiting
Our friend and fearless high school class leader who
kept all of us connected over the years and inspired us
with his defiant, yet graceful, exit from this earth.

CONTENTS

INTRODUCTION

A couple of years ago, my niece passed away. Although she had been clean and sober for some years, her previous alcohol and drug addiction had taken its toll. I wrote a verse in her memory, and the tone seemed a bit somber, so I wrote a second, more positive verse. Then I embarked on a year of writing—not every day, but when I thought of something to write about.

This is the result. I do not aspire to call this poetry. These are simply my life observations, written in verse form. I was hopeful of incorporating some universality into the writing. I will let you decide whether I have succeeded.

Friendly Fire[1]

The so-called friendly fire
was certainly not friendly,
but it was fire.
Fire from the
depths of Hell,
with the swaggering
God of War,
stretching forth his
long-reaching, ruthless
Hand of Eternity,
Grabbing the Children
Whose future
could-have-beens
and would-have-beens
were now scattered on
the wind called Nevermore.

When he enlisted
he had handed over a signed,
blank check.
The amount due,
later filled in,
consisted of two simple words:
Your life.
It is now stamped:
Paid in full.

---

[1]   http://www.virtualwall.org/iStates.htm

They say there are lessons
to be learned from war.
They say many things.
For talk is cheap.

The Gargoyle

Perched atop these smooth,
beautiful stones
here I have sat for
hundreds of years,
surveying the city,
breathing in the sights,
the sounds, the lights,
and relishing my part in it.

Peering down at all the people
looking up.
Flash, flash, flash…
How I loved having
my picture taken.
Look at me. Look at me.
Here I am.
Do you see me?

Did they see how hard
I was working.

How hard *we* were working
to watch over Our Lady.

Watching.
Always watching.
On guard.
Looking. Listening.
But then it happened.
The fire and flames leaped so quickly.
I cried out.
We all cried out.
Attencion: Warning, warning.
Danger, danger.
Help us please.
Please save Our Lady.
Please save us.
The flames are too hot.
They are burning us.
The tears that stream from our eyes
go unseen,
vaporizing in the blaze.

But look: They've heard us!
The people are hurrying,
Running, screaming, frantic.
Grabbing and carrying.
Rushing in, rushing out.
They save many things.

Can they save us?
For we are only made of stone.

Tina's Retrospective

We come through the door
into the unknown.
We embark on this life's journey.
Life—
An unforgiving, unrelenting teacher.
My Family—
Did I forget to tell my Parents
and my Brothers
How much I love then?
So many regrets.
My Children—
I did the best I could.
I think that it was not enough.
And yet…
I see their wings.
They have learned to fly.
I smile at many good memories.
Life's journey—
We walk. We stumble. We fall.
We get up again. We go on.
Too soon it is over.
The door slowly closes.
Night settles in.

FOR TINA

I opened the door of destiny,
and blithely walked on through.
It was only on the other side
that I learned a thing or two.

Regrets, mistakes, I had them all.
Indeed they were rolled up in a ball.
It bounced hard as I threw it down,
then sprang back up, my thoughts to drown.

But here I am on the other side.
Why was I so afraid of the tide?
It washed me clean, as you can see,
and I stand now with Eternity.

She smiles as we walk hand in hand.
The hourglass no longer filled with sand.
The addictions are gone. Can it really be?
Thank God, at last, I am truly free.

THE WORLD LISTENING

He said the wrong things.
He criticized the wrong people.
He thought the wrong thoughts.
He used to hang around with
the wrong people—
until they became
the right people,
and quit associating with him.
Until they
turned him in.

Now here he was
on the row.
Death row.
The place to be
for people like him.
People who thought wrong:
Dangerous thinkers.

No more would he say
the wrong things.
No more would he criticize
the wrong people.
No more would he share
his wrong thoughts.
Now the world resounded
In his silence.
In the silence.

THE VISIT

The torrent of tears
that flooded his face
as she said
I forgive you
was contagious.
Now here she was
sobbing,
hugging the man
who had caused
such pain.

The bridge of forgiveness
was now built.
The road here
had not been easy.
Is any road ever easy?
But she had made it.
She was happy.
He was happy.

The visit
was soon over.
As she said goodbye
and the metal doors
clanged shut,
she walked forward
in beauty and grace,

and now, at last,
in freedom.

And what about him?
Like his tears,
her freedom
had been contagious.

THE WAITING ROOM

The Old Man:
Quiet. Alone.
Sitting. Waiting and waiting.
And more waiting.

Please do not waste my time,
for I am almost out of time.
Or so you said…
What have you said?
That I am terminal? Of what?
Of life?
But wasn't it always so.

An unguarded tear
falls from his eye.
Oh, to have just one more year.
What I would give.
I beg of you. I'm pleading.
Please God.
Can you hear me?
Are you listening?
I promise I'll do better.
I promise, I promise.
Please God.
Can you hear me?
Are you there?

Suddenly the bright morning sun
discovers the old man's face.

An unseen hand cradles his fall.

THE LADY IN WHITE

Drip, drip, drip.
Golden liquid pulsing
into clear, plastic tubing.
Mesmerizing and somehow calming
to the young child
tethered to its destination.
Head balding, body shrinking,
spirit indomitable.
Thoughts clear and focused,
looking inward and outward.

The child's parents
failing in their attempt
at gaiety.
How can she tell them
about the visit?
About the Lady who visited
last night,
dressed in blazing white light?

Do not fear.
for I will safely guide you home
she said…
Many years from now.

Childhood Games

It was recess and my friend and I played.
My childhood dreams had not yet been frayed.
Then she asked me a question
that in my heart caught:
Mother wants to know whether you are Indian
or not.
For Mother says we cannot play
if the answer is yes. What do you say?

What could I say. I was only a child.
At life's seeming illusions
I had been beguiled.

When her mom picked her up that bright,
sunny day,
a cloud crossed her face
as she looked my way.

We never played together again.
There were no more games
at childhood's end.

THE ROCK

We're here
near the mountaintop,
reveling in this day
of blue skies, warm breezes,
and a brilliant sun.
This high up,
we're surrounded mostly
by stones and rocks.

Our gaze had gravitated
to one particular rock.
There was something
unique
about that one rock,
nestled among
a quarry of rocks.
We wondered
what it would say
if it could talk.
What tales would it tell.

We asked,
and we were listening
as sleep crept towards us.
Then we heard it:
not a sound,
but a sensing, a knowing.

Indeed
the rock had
many stories to tell.
Stories
of loss and love,
of ignorance and wisdom
of sounds and silence,
of beginnings and endings.

Mostly though
it rejoiced in the memory
of being pushed
in front of the cave
and then being rolled away.
The joy of that moment
radiating in its being
now
and forever.

Peruvian Memory

Pouncing pumas,
soft forms
stealthily gliding
against ancient stones.
The towering, charcoal stones,
standing as Warriors,
interlocked, in step.

Giant beings
forever gracing our hearts.
Old souls.
Briefly permitting
a glimpse of yesterday,
a glance at tomorrow.

MY FRIEND NU

We spoke different languages
and yet here we were
roommates in a Las Vegas hotel.
Her name was Nu,
my best friend's mother.
How would we get along,
I wondered.
I like my room warm—
not freezing cold.
As it turned out,
Nu also liked the room warm.

As we went to bed
that first evening,
Nu turned on the light in the bathroom,
and left it on.
Had she read my mind?
That's exactly what I always do.
No bumping into things
in the middle of the night.

Over the years
we shared a room and many
New Year's Eve weekends
together
in Las Vegas.

As we got to know each other,
we settled into an easy routine.

We would sit at the small round table
and leisurely eat our breakfast.
We would chat with each other,
she speaking in Vietnamese
and me in English.
We were always smiling,
even laughing.
Our words entered the quiet space
and swirled and mingled
in the air above and around us.
Our words were foreign
to each other,
but their translation
was simple, unmistakable,
and understood completely:

The message was love.

On November 1st
Nu took a walk
with the Angels.

How I miss you,
my dear, sweet Nu.

THE CHILD

Sleep is overpowering me.
In just a few minutes
it will be all over.
The pain—
gone for good.

No more needlessly asking,
Why me?
Why, Mom, why?
Why didn't you help me?
Why didn't you protect me?
Why wasn't I more
important to you?
Was it my fault?
Was I not good enough?
Why, Mommie, why?

Endless questions.
Endless guesses
at the answer.
At an answer.
Any answer.
There is no answer.
Only questions.
incessant questions…

And so I shall sleep
the Big Sleep.

Author's note:

As Tony Robbins, a well-known motivational speaker, might say,

This young person could be empowered to ask a better question, and view the experience in a self-empowering, rather than a destructive light.

Better questions might be:

What can I learn from this?

Can this experience help me to grow?

How can I use this experience to help others?

LIONESS

She had gone along
with their pettiness,
their arrogance,
and their feigned superiority
because she wanted to belong.
It was comforting
and exhilarating
To be part of the in-crowd.

But then one day
Her "friends" began taunting
a young girl.
The Golden Rule
had gotten lost
under piles of ego
run amok.
Caught cold,
the Lioness sloughed off
her winter sleep.
The roar was heard
throughout the land.

The Lioness
saying goodbye to winter,
and forming a new Pride,
had found her voice.

She had gotten feedback:
The voice
was catching fire.

THE VOYAGE HOME

The sea was calm
as we got in my boat.
Out to the island
we thought we would float.

The trip over was nice,
but was there a price
to be paid to life's Master
for we soon courted disaster.

As we headed back
the blue skies turned black.
The rain was not nice
and began pelting like ice.

Then our little boat went under
after the peal of the thunder.
How could we not drown
for the waves pulled us down.

The struggle was fierce,
and our minds did it pierce.
And then it was done.
The battle was won.

There were no more scars
as we rode through the stars.

MOTHER

The container with
the ashes
is still sitting
on the shelf
where we placed it
several years ago.
The contents still waiting
to be scattered
over the mountain,
as you had wished.
The ashes swirling and dancing
with the wind,
blown here and there,
and dropping into Eternity.

We are your overachievers
who take pride in getting things done
quickly and efficiently.
And yet
this simple task eludes us.

Dear Mother,
please forgive your
greedy children
who just want
to hang on to you.

ETHEREAL BIRD

The stones hit and bounced off
the beautiful bird.
Big stones, little stones,
round stones, jagged stones.
Too many stones to count.
Too many days and weeks
to even remember
when it began
or why it began.
Negative forces—seemingly everywhere.
Was not his voice
their voice?
Was not his truth
their truth?
Was not his song
their song?
His heart said yes.
The stones said no.

The road had been long.
Now he is weary.
His body is battered.
His head is bruised.
His heart is heavy.
He teeters and sways.

But then he sees them.
Thousands, no millions of people
coming towards him,
blocking the stones,
catching the stones,
stopping the stones.

They are supporting him,
helping him,
lifting him up.
Now he can breathe.
Now he can think.
Now he can remember.
Yes, now he remembers.
This is his land.
This is his country.
These are his people.

They would help him remember
how to fly.
And he would teach them
to soar.

THE WALK

For Joseph Timothy "Tim" Whiting

The early morning hike
was usually with Friends,
but today he walked
in solitude.
The gentle sound of the
flowing creek
sang in harmony
with cascading memories:
What a grand life!
So many friends—
too many to count—
for he was a Connector.
His former classmates
were now emailing each other,
sharing funny, heartfelt
stories and memories.
He was the friend and
fearless leader
who had kept everyone together
these many years.
He felt a modest pride in that.

He had been to many places.
He had many more places to go.
There were so many
grand adventures

just awaiting.
Where to, what next?

Just as he was pondering
the possibilities,
the tree,
gently swaying and
shimmering through
the Mists of Forever,
beckoned to him.
The birds hushed
their singing.

And as he walked
into the forest,
the Angels
drew him near.

THE UNDER TOAD

The water so calm,
the Under Toad so frisky,
I wanted to play
even though it seemed risky.

Come over, he said,
there's nothing to dread.
You will not drown,
We'll just frolic around. And around.
And around…

FREEDOM

Locked cell,
Free mind—
Unlimited universe.

Making It

I didn't know
that I could make it,
until I made it.

Whoever you are,
wherever you are,
you've got it.
You've made it!

WORDS SPOKEN

I forgive you.
Three simple words—
Two people freed.

THE DOOR

A beautiful golden door
beckons you:
Come within,
you are waiting.

Sounds of Silence

An ancient bell
breaks the silence,
its sounds cascading
to nothingness.

THE LABYRINTH

Walking the labyrinth
I come full circle:
inner and outer
are one.

Her Time

She senses that it is
almost her time
to cross into
the Future.

Why so soon.
Why so soon.
Who will know
that she was here.
Who will know.
Who will know…

My Friends

My Friends
had a birthday party;
they forgot
to invite me.

Ouch

All the various slights
and little snubs
that have accosted me
are filed away
in my mind
under a category
called "Ouch."

Mystery Solved

Who took my toilet paper?
All of the shelves are empty.
But the mystery is quickly solved.
Masked bandits all around me…

THE RACE[2]

It was their Olympics,
their race.
They had trained hard.
Up early, daily exercising,
daily running and more running.
Training their muscles.
Going faster.
Covering more ground
in less time.

And today was the day.
This was their race.
How fast could they go?
Would their coaches be happy?
Would their parents be proud?
Who would win?
A thousand thoughts and dreams
at the starting gun.

The starting gun snaps the air.

And now everyone is running,
legs pumping, hearts pounding,
rounding the second corner,
rounding the third corner,
rounding the fourth corner.

---

2   For, and inspired by, the Children of the Special Olympics.

There's the home stretch.
The finish line is in sight.

Then catastrophe.
Suddenly Bobby is down.
Knees skinned, ankle twisted,
dreams shattered.

Then almost as suddenly,
the race leader stops.
All the runners stop.
They go back to Bobby.
He is carefully lifted up.

Supporting and carrying Bobby,
the runners cross the finish line—
Together.

After all,
This was *their* race.
The human race.

About the Author

Barbara Larson Webb is an Alaskan Native who was born and raised in Juneau, Alaska. She went to undergraduate and graduate school in Colorado, where she fell in love with all of the abundant sunshine, and decided to stay. She lives in Denver, Colorado, with her husband, John Webb, a former judge on the Colorado Court of Appeals.